CHRIST JESUS THE ROCK

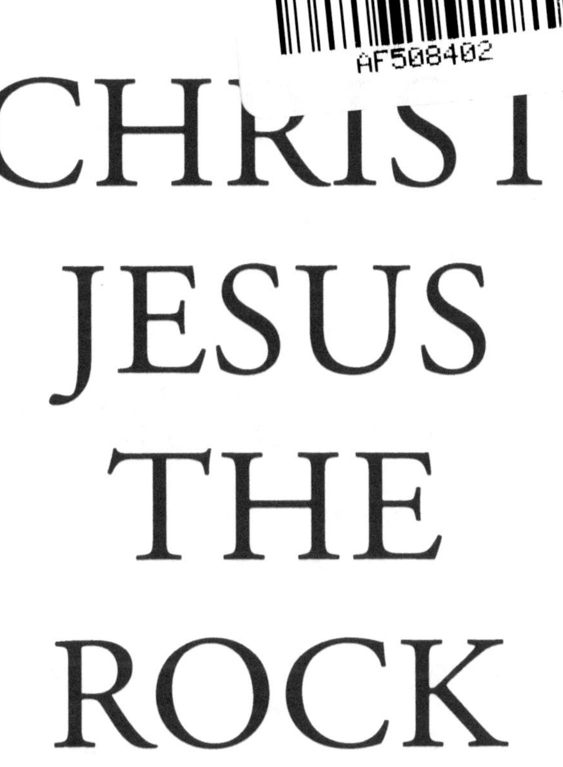

An adventure through the Old and
New Testament
Tracing the identification of God as
"The Rock of Israel."

Merle Cooper and Charlotte Cooper

ISBN 979-8-89112-112-6 (Paperback)
ISBN 979-8-89112-113-3 (Digital)

All Bible references are from the New International Version.

Covenant Books
11661 Hwy 707
Murrells Inlet, SC 29576
www.covenantbooks.com

INTRODUCTION

Who Do You Say That I Am?

In the last culminating days of his life on Earth, the cross looming near, Jesus put this question to Peter. It is the central question that a person must answer.

Jesus said, "Who do you say that I am?"

Peter answered, "You are the Christ, the Son of the Living God."

And Jesus answered him saying, "Blessed are you, Simon, son of Jonah, for flesh and blood has not revealed this to you, but my Father in heaven and I tell you, you are Peter and on this rock I will build my church." (Matthew 16:13–18)

From that declaration, a certain amount of confusion has ensued. What did Jesus mean by "this rock"? Did he mean Peter was the foundation of the church? Many have thought so. Or was it the idea itself—that Jesus is the Son of God? And if so, why did Jesus then change his disciple's name from Cephas to Petros, which wasn't even a Hebrew or Aramaic name, but rather the Greek word for *rock*?

For many, the statement is puzzling, a perplexing declaration, a riddle. But while we may be confused, Peter probably was not. Jesus's statement would have had the ring of truth and recognition for him. It would have been the last puzzle piece set exactly in place, the dawning of the *great understanding*, and the comprehension of the presence of God within us—Emmanuel.

In order to see the truth of this great affirmation as clearly as Jesus's disciples did, we need to know what they knew and step into the context of Peter's world. Let us try to see what any ordinary observant first-century Jew would have known on the significance of the *rock*.

When we know what Jesus meant—and what Peter understood—by "this rock," we can understand the most basic idea about Christ. In the same way that we know that the Earth revolves around the sun (and not as people assumed for so long, the other way around), Peter knew that Jesus was God—the underlying reality of all existence, the foundation, and the rock.

This is a quest, a mystery to be uncovered, clue by clue. It takes us from the old father, Jacob, blessing his long-lost son Joseph, through the wilderness

CHRIST JESUS THE ROCK

First Six-Week Session

Introduction: Who do you say that I am?

Week 1
Genesis 49:22–25

The Shepherd, the Rock of Israel
Jacob knew what it was to live in the grip of greed and deceit. Turning to God as the underlying reality and guide (shepherd) is his prayer/blessing for his son and for us.

Week 2
Exodus 33:21–22
Deuteronomy 32:4–5
Deuteronomy 32:15–18

"Show me your Glory"
A God who shows us his glory while he shields us from the intensity.

Week 3
John 7:37–39
Exodus 17:5–6
Numbers 20:8–12

Water from the Rock
Jesus identifies the water from the living rock in the wilderness with himself, the source of life. (This is the central study in the series.)

Week 4
2 Samuel 22:1–4, 32, 47
2 Samuel 23:3
Psalm 18: 2, 31, 46

David's Rock
A study full of praise as David glimpses the glory of the one who supports him in the present and who is to come.

Week 5–8

Other Psalms and Other Singers
Psalms 18:1–4, 28:1, 31:3, 40:2, 62:2, 71:3, 94:22, 105:41, 114:8, all songs and all praises that celebrate the solid rock. A chance to make this praise our own.

Week 6
Daniel 2:28, 2:34, 35
2:20, 22

The Rock That Filled
the Whole Earth
Daniel has a vision for
the rock that destroys
the prevailing political
powers (Babylon,
present-day Iraq) and
fills the whole earth!

CHAPTER 1

THE SHEPHERD, THE ROCK OF ISRAEL

"Joseph is a fruitful bough,
a fruitful bough by a spring,
his branches run over the wall.
The archers fiercely attacked him,
They shot at him and pressed him hard.
Yet his bough remained taut
And his arms were made agile
By the hands of the Mighty One of Jacob,
By the name of the Shepherd,
The Rock of Israel,
By the God of your father, who will help you
By the Almighty, who will bless you
With blessings of heaven above,
Blessings of the deep that lies beneath."
—Genesis 49:22–25
Blessings of the deep
that lies beneath NIV

Jacob, son of Isaac, grandson of Abraham, father of Joseph and all the brothers, used it first: the *rock* of Israel.

Jacob said it first, but the name was used by ancient Hebrew writers again and again to refer to Yahweh, God Almighty. The rock—it means, of course, a great deal more than a chunk of granite or limestone. No formal definition exists for the term, but the meaning is made clear by the usage. And this is what we need to know. When and why was the God of Israel called "the rock"?

Jacob, old and foolish, had come to the final days of his life. The long journey was over—the long years when he thought his beloved son Joseph was dead and the long years when his other sons lived with the awful secret that they had sold their brother into slavery. Joseph was discovered, safe, and prosperous in in Egypt. The family was together at last.

As he lay dying, Jacob gathered his great family, the beginning of the tribe of Israel, and told him what he saw ahead. Most of his sons had disappointed him, and what he had to say about them was grim, but when he came to Joseph, the son who had been faithful even as a slave, Jacob blessed him.

Jacob was the son God had promised Isaac, the child of his beloved Rachel. Jacob's first ten sons were the children of Jacob's conniving days and of a wife foisted on him by trickery—and they reflected this in their character. They sold their younger, preferred brother right into the hands of slave traders.

Joseph had lived in Egypt his whole adult life. Probably he had not heard the name of Yahweh in all that time. Instead, he had been surrounded by the wealth and power of the greatest nation in the ancient world and by their gods.

But Joseph was still in the path of God's blessing; he was able to receive the blessing his father wanted to give. That day, Jacob blessed Joseph with "the blessings of the deep," the wonderful reality that the destiny of the tribe of Joseph rested on the one who underlies all creation and not on what appeared to be powerful around him.

The great cities of northern Egypt, where Joseph was a government administrator, were located in a wide delta that was flooded every year by the Nile River. When Jacob, fleeing the famine in Canaan, arrived with his family, they had no idea that they would stay to become slaves of the Egyptians. It would prove to be a spiritual swamp as well as a geological one. The prevailing wisdom was that, of course, here were many gods and that the Pharoah was a living king/god who became fully divine upon his death. This culture would dominate the Israelites for generations to come. It would be four hundred years before God would raise up Moses to lead them home again.

Meanwhile, old Jacob was blessing his son, and what he said was that he had already been blessed by the hand of the shepherd, the *rock* of Israel.

Jacob's understanding of God had its limits. He knew that God was great, and he knew that he was holy. He was so holy that you weren't even supposed to say his name. (But he probably didn't yet have the idea that there is only one God.) He knew that Yahweh promised to care for Israel. He called him "shepherd," and he didn't mean a man. He called him "rock," and he didn't mean a monument. It was a solid start.

A few questions for this week:

How are you shaped by the "powers" of the world we live in?

What part of your life feels like a swamp to you?

What effect would it have to count on the shepherd, the rock of our salvation, instead of anything else (such as financial security, social connections, and personal control of things)? What changes would take place?

How would you bless your children? What would you say as you think of them as God's people, and not just your children?

CHAPTER 2

"Show Me Your Glory"

"See, there is a place by me where you shall stand on the rock while my glory passes by, I will put you in a cleft of the rock and I will cover you with my hand until I have passed by."
—Exodus 33:21–22 NIV

Yosemite was full of crashing water. It was late spring after a winter of record rain, and snowfall and all the rivers were swollen and rushing. The waterfalls were exploding over the cliffs and rocky ledges.

We—two parents, two grandparents, and two small children—were climbing to Vernal Falls, 1.7 steep miles beside a raging river.

Jacob, adventurous at four, kept up easily. He talked all the way. The climb was harder for two-year-old Johnny, but he was determined. "I do it myself," he muttered as he trudged his small, two-year-old steps beside our longer ones.

He almost made it, but near the end of the climb, he gave out. He finished the hike on his father's shoulders, fast asleep.

At the top of the trail is a sturdy bridge, spanning a gorge with rocks the size of small trucks and a rush of water powerful enough to move them around. It churned like an enormous, sunlit, washing machine, and it roared like a jet, a wild orgy of power. We grabbed Jacob's hand and held on tight.

Across the bridge, Johnny's parents were sitting on boulders the size of sofas, unwrapping sandwiches and fruit bars. Between them, nestled in his father's jacket, in a nook in the rocks, lay Johnny, fast asleep. A baseball cap lay over his face to shade him from the sun, but you could see that he was smiling in his sleep.

He lay there most of the hour while we lunched and sunned ourselves. The terrible power, the rushing torrent a few yards away didn't concern him at all. He was safe in his parents' care, asleep in the cleft of the rock.

The account of Moses begging to see God's glory is a difficult story, and most of us get it wrong. We think it's the story in the Sunday school papers, but it's not. Moses's story and his longing to see God is something desperate—and full of glory.

It is four hundred years after the time of Jacob. Egypt, the same nation which gave refuge to the starving tribe, has turned them into slaves. They have been in captivity almost the entire time. But although their lives have been hard, the descendants of Jacob have grown into a multitude.

We join them on the journey in the wilderness. In fact, the occasion is the giving of the Covenant—the Ten Commandments—the first time.

Moses had been slow in coming down from his encounter with the Lord on the mountain. The Hebrew people brought up in the culture of Egypt, where many gods are thought to exist, had begun to lose their nerve. They were not sure it was a good idea to trust in the old god of their forefathers.

After all, they had been the slaves, and their Egyptian masters had prospered and ruled. So it stood to reason that the Egyptian gods must have been stronger. So the children of Israel hedged their bets; they collected enough gold to melt down and cast the image of an old fertility idol—a golden calf. It was something solid, something they could see.

Moses came down from the mountain with the tablets in his hands. They were engraved by the hand of God. We don't know what characters were used, but it was something Moses could read and understand. Before he could get down the mountain, the Lord alerted him to what the people were doing.

Moses was in a rage. He smashed the tablets and confronted Aaron, who said, "The people gave me their gold, and I threw it into the fire and out came this calf!"

There followed a terrible trial by ordeal, in which Moses smashed the idol, ground it into powder under his heel, and then mixed it with water and made the Israelites—those who are standing there with Aaron—drink it.

Then Moses stood in the gate of the camp and said (he must have yelled), "Who is on the Lord's side! Come to me!" (Exodus 32:26 NIV).

The Levites, those of Moses own tribe, came and were sent to kill each one—his relative, his neighbor, his friend, among the revelers. About three thousand people fell that day, and the wild party stopped. Lastly, the Lord sent sudden, catastrophic illnesses on those who drank the metal mixed with water. The idolatry and insurrection were put down.

The anger of the Lord raged on.

"Let me alone," he said, "And I will consume them."

Moses argued desperately with the Lord, reminding him of his promises and begging him not to destroy the Israelites. And God listened to the man he called his friend. He withheld his hand.

The next day, in sober disappointment, Moses approached the Lord once more.

"Go, just go," said the Lord. "And take those people *you* brought with you. I will keep my promises, but I won't go with you. If, for a single moment," said the Lord, "I did go among you, I would consume you, like a fire too intense to approach, like a laser beam, like a million volts of electricity."

The people, sober and ashamed by this time, mourned. Like a beautiful woman who is shattered by humiliation, they took off all their ornaments. From that time on, it was a somber multitude.

It is easy to assume that Moses went up the mountain and got the second set of commandments forth with, but a careful reading indicates that some time passed. There was a long time when the Lord refused to have anything to do with the people. They waited in their tents, and the presence of the Lord was not among them.

Those were dark days. The people had lost the joyful trust and the edge of courage with which they had first followed Moses.

Meanwhile, outside the camp, Moses set up a tent where he went to meet God. The people came to the door of their tents and watched as Moses passed, an old man, half defeated, hoping, and fearing to meet God in the tabernacle. And God did indeed meet Moses there, and the scripture says that they spoke face-to-face as friends speak.

But Moses was frustrated for more. "Show me your glory," he said to God. "I want to see you, yourself."

There are people who are drunk with the notion of God: the Hasidic, whirling in holy joy; certain Pentecostal believers, collapsing in ecstasy. Moses was one of these. He glimpsed the presence of the Lord; he was dazzled, and he yearned for more.

Like the other refugees from Egypt, Moses had also grown up in an atmosphere absolutely suffused with polytheism—the idea of many gods. Every person in Egypt knew about Ra, Isis, and Osiris, the god of the underworld. When Moses said, "Tell me your name," he was asking a question that came out of this background.

But Moses was also a man who had some glimpse of the Holy One. He had seen him in the burning bush and heard the voice who said, "I Am." He had seen what the Lord did in sending the plagues on Egypt and on parting the waters for the great escape. The pillar of smoke by day and fire by night—the evidence of the Lord—went with him in the wilderness. What more did Moses want?

Moses wanted what someone who loves wants. He wanted to know the person of God! He called it glory.

And the Lord said, "I will make my goodness pass before you, and I will proclaim before you the name, YHWH." And he did.

So hidden in a crack in the rock, God's hand over him, Moses glimpsed the back of God.

But what rock is safe enough to shelter a man from the terrifying Glory of God? Not for another thousand years will that question have an answer.

God's goodness seems to be a defining quality. Baal and Ashteroth, gods whom the Israelites assumed to be real, were thought to be powerful, but no one called them "good." People felt they had to protect themselves from these forces.

But Yahweh was known to be good, to be holy. And that, as it turns out, is the problem. Holiness is such a burning force that human beings (not as "good" as they once thought) are destroyed by it, unless they are hidden in the cleft of a *rock*.

So is this the Christ? Or is it just a rock, protecting Moses from nothing more than heat or light? Certainly, Messiah was present in that time ("before Abraham was and I am"). And what Moses had to be sheltered from was the holiness—the goodness of God.

It isn't important to answer all the questions that emerge at this point. What is important is to consider what happened to Moses. He was hidden in the rock to remember it. As Peter and the other Jews of his time did.

Much later, just before he died, Moses sang a song of warning and regret. In Deuteronomy, we read:

> "The Rock, his work is perfect
> and all his ways are just,
> A faithful God without deceit,
> just and upright is he,
> yet his degenerate children
> have dealt falsely with him,
> a perverse and crooked generation."
> (Deuteronomy 32:4–5)

> "Jacob (the family of Jacob) ate his
>   fill…
> he abandoned the God who made
>   him
> and scoffed at the Rock of his
>   salvation.
> They made him jealous with strange
>   gods,
> with abhorrent things they provoked
>   him,
> and scoffed at the Rock of his
>   salvation.
> They sacrificed to demons, not to
>   God,
> to deities they had never known,
> to new ones, recently arrived,
> whom their ancestors had not known.
> You were unmindful of the Rock that
>   bore you;
> you forgot the God who gave you
>   birth."
> (Deuteronomy 32:15–18 NIV)

Notice the parallel form of poetry. An idea is expressed twice, sometimes three times, in slightly differing form. It's a poetic device that translates smoothly. It also helps to clarify things; if you don't get it one way, there is a second chance.

Notice also that in verse 17, the "other gods"—and there were many—were not just fakes or other pathways to God; they were demons.

All through this tirade, the "rock" means Yahweh, and "rock" sometimes means a false god.

Verse 31 says, "Indeed their rock is not like our Rock." And verse 37 says, "Then he will say, 'Where are their gods, the rock in which they took refuge?'"

Counterfeits abound.

Task:

What glimpses of God's goodness and glory have I seen?

In what ways does Jesus shelter us from the holiness of God?

Do I need to be protected from God?

CHAPTER 3

Water from the Rock

"Jesus stood in the city square and shouted,
'Let anyone who is thirsty come to me!
Let the one who believes in me drink!
Out of the believer's heart
shall flow rivers of living water!"
—John 7:37–39 NIV

Jesus stood in the public square and *roared* this claim at the top of his voice, and every Jew there heard it, and they heard it in the context of their history—the water that gushed from the rock in the wilderness.

Now, consider the account of Moses striking the rock in the wilderness. There are two witnesses, two views.

Both stories begin with an argument and with a terrible thirst. In the wilderness account, they had run out of water. The people and the animals are desperate. In the rocky desert, death by dehydra-

18

tion was stalking them. It was just a matter of hours before the old people and the little children would begin to drop, and the lambs and kids.

In both accounts, the people argued with Moses, and they failed to trust God. In fact, the root of their quarrel, once more, was, "Is God really among us?" They were not sure that he was. And they regret leaving the "safety" of Egypt. It seemed easier to be a slave sometimes than to trust in God's care. They would like proof of that.

Exodus gives the bare bones of the story:

> The Lord said to Moses, "Go ahead of the people and take in your hand the rod with which you struck the Nile, and go. I will be standing there in front of you on the rock at Horeb. Strike the rock and water will come out of it, so that the people may drink." (Exodus 17:5–6 NIV)

East of Red Bluff, in the middle of a barren northern California valley, there is water—a lake—where no other water is, for miles and miles around. No river runs into it. It is just there. Why? There is a broad rock, one of the largest shelves of limestone on the continent, and the water runs under it from Shasta Lake, in the mountains, and miles to the north. At the site of the lake, the rock tips, and the water flows to the surface—an artesian lake.

Consider this rock in the wilderness. You couldn't hold it in your hand; it's not the size of a bread box or even a Volkswagen. It's the limestone substructure of the whole area. They have been on this rock for most of the wilderness trek. They have been walking on it. Their sheep have been walking on it. It's the underlying geographical feature. Where Moses was to strike it, it probably looked like a wall to them, and underneath was water.

Now consider the water. It didn't flow like a faucet being turned on. Probably there was a gush of water that knocked people down and got everybody wet and made mud all over. There was water to drink and water for washing, and very likely, that night, in the damp woolen tents, there was the ripe smell of wet wool, wet goats, and wet sheep.

This was the place where God showed his care by giving them water, but Moses named it "test" and "fault finding." The anxiety and the wrangling of the people pushed out the joy and thankfulness that could have been.

The account in Numbers tells us more about how it went. There was no water, so the people organized and went to Moses and complained bitterly and long. They complained about leaving the security of captivity, about leaving the place they knew. Moses, and now Aaron with him, got away and went to the tent of meeting and fell on their faces. The glory of the Lord appeared to them.

In Numbers 20:8–12, this is what he said:

"Take the staff and assemble the congregation, you and your brother Aaron and command the rock before their eyes to yield its water. Thus you shall bring water out of the rock for them, thus you shall provide drink for the congregation and their livestock."

So Moses took the staff from before the Lord, as he had commanded him. Moses and Aaron gathered the assembly together before the rock and he said to them, "Listen, you rebels, shall we bring water for you out of this rock?"

Then Moses lifted up his hand and struck the rock twice with his staff, water came out abundantly and the congregation and their livestock drank.

But the Lord said to Moses and Aaron, "Because you did not trust in me, to show my holiness before the eyes of the Israelites, therefore you shall not bring this assembly into the land that I have given them."

This narrative identifies the place by the name "Meribah," which means "quarreling." Moses, caught up in the quarrel, in anger and frustration, and to show of whatever power he had, hit the rock instead of speaking to it. And the water flowed. But there was quarreling there and mistrust.

Both versions say, "Take the staff—the one that Moses used to part the Red Sea." Exodus says that the Lord said to strike the rock, but Numbers says he was to command it, and probably, this was the original direction. Striking it was a compromise with a heavy consequence.

What difference could it have made that Moses struck the rock instead of speaking to it? It was a desperate situation. They were all in extreme need of water. The herders among them, experienced in the harsh realities of nomadic life, knew their flocks, and they knew the flocks and the families couldn't last much longer.

Modern guides in this part of the world tell of occasional flash floods that burst across the rocky wilderness, coursing between and under out-croppings of boulders and other rock formations. Sometimes, water gets trapped in there, in some hidden cul-de-sac.

An experienced desert dweller will walk through clusters of rock, hitting them with a heavy stick and occasionally dislodging a pocket of trapped water in this way. Moses made the sovereign act of God look like the result of primitive human technology.

It was a lapse in belief in the power of God and in his intervention in their lives. Can the Lord save? Is he "among us" as he said?

At that moment, Moses wasn't sure, and in his anger and frustration, he added his own action to the command of God.

For this lack of trust, he himself would not be trusted to lead the people into the Promised Land. It was a bitter price to pay for a spiritual failure of nerve.

Still, this is one of those passages that is troublesome until you put it next to what Jesus said in John 7, the words he shouted in the public square on the last day of Passover, just before the crucifixion. (He said this about the Spirit.)

> "Let anyone who is thirsty, come to
> me.
> Let the one who believes in me drink!
> And out of the believers' heart shall
> flow rivers of living water."

Jesus speaks in Old Testament images. Before their eyes, prophecy and promise become reality. In fact, during the seven days of Passover, it was the custom to bring water in a golden bowl from the Pool of Siloam to the temple. It was a symbol of the water from the rock and of the hope of the coming Messiah.

The signs were not obscure; they were part of the fabric of Jewish life. Now, before them, instead of the hope, was the reality—Messiah, the deliverer. Jesus claimed the symbol.

It is a seamless whole.

Yahweh, in glory in the wilderness, asked Moses not to do magic or some primitive technology with a heavy stick and an unstable fault line, but to *ask* for water.

Messiah, in human form, said, "Come! Believe! Drink!"

It is all the same thing. It is all the same one!

CHAPTER 4

David's Rock

"The Lord is my Rock, my
fortress and my deliverer,
my God, my rock, in whom I take refuge."

"The Lord lives! Blessed be my rock,
and exalted be my God, the rock of my salvation."
—2 Samuel 22:3, 47 NIV

We live in place so flat that if you never saw any other landscape, you couldn't even believe in mountains. Country that was diagonal and even vertical would seem impossible.

But even here, beyond the miles of flatness, there is a glimpse of something else. On a very clear day, you can see the snow-draped Sierra Nevada, off on the horizon, a small ridge, far away. But as you drive closer, that small spine becomes a world of mountains that vault into the sky, where the air changes, grows colder, thinner, and takes your breath away.

It's good to live in the vicinity of mountains to be reminded that the Earth we walk on is not always moderate in its configuration.

Every year, our family camps in Yosemite. For a week, we camp in that narrow valley where the cliffs rise straight up around us. We are in a slot in the mountain range within the landscape, instead of merely on top of it.

All around us, the cliffs rise, vaulting straight up to amazing heights. We forget flatness.

One late night, we rode through Yosemite Valley in the back of an open bed truck. We were waiting for the moon to rise. We saw the moonlight first on the sheer face of the great massif, El Capitan, in a wash of silver and dark steel.

That great cliff rises straight up into the drifting clouds. Here and there, on the dark face of it, we saw lights. They were the lanterns of climbers. The driver turned off the engine, and in the quiet, we called back and forth to the climbers hanging on the face of the cliff. They sleep where they climb, in hammocks secured by pitons to the rock.

But even these awesome mountains are only a flimsy hint of the *rock* we consider here. Even these rocks, solid as they may appear, are changing and unreliable.

One summer day, high above the head of the valley, a boulder, worn by the erosion of countless centuries, shifted a little and broke away. It hit the valley floor like a bomb exploding. At impact, pines were uprooted and flung like shrapnel. A camper died when one of these trees hit him.

The boulder itself was smashed to dust as thick as fog. The smell of granite hung in the valley for weeks.

A rock is only a picture; the reality is greater. David's rock, the Lord, is a shelter, a deliverer.

So David sang a song of praise, a victory shout of a man who had survived a powerful enemy.

There had been a series of battles with the Philistines. The Philistines were bigger and better armed than David's men. One of them was a man of unusual size, with six fingers on each hand and six toes on each foot. One man had a spear the size of a weaver's beam, a shaft that would normally take two men to carry.

But the battle was won, and David knew why. His world, though often embattled, was not seriously shaken; the Lord was his fortress, his place of safety. The Lord was also the underlying significance of David's life. Nothing, nothing, meant anything without him.

The Psalms sing the same song—the song of security in the midst of trouble.

Psalm 18:2, 31, 46 NIV are a good example:

> "I love you, O Lord, my strength
> The Lord is my Rock, my fortress, my
> deliverer,

my God, my Rock in whom I take
refuge,
my shield, my stronghold."

It is the same song recorded in 2 Samuel.

Years later, when David lay dying, he again called God the rock of Israel (2 Samuel 23:3). He was secure.

Remember, "rock" is a representation of an idea. This was never about actual stones. It's not even a picture of unfailing protection or reliability, like the insurance company logo of the Rock of Gibraltar. It's something much more than that. It was a way to think about enormous underlying reality. It is reality so basic it is sometimes hard to see or talk about.

David, that great sinner and great man of faith, used the name "rock" in a very personal way. He sang his praise for the one whom he called "my rock."

What Jacob glimpsed and what was revealed more fully to Moses, David lived by. It was personal. He sang it. He cheered it.

"Blessed be my Rock!" The presence of God was the underlying reality of his life.

Jacob believed, but he lived by his own devices.

Moses was a hesitant believer and a great complainer.

But David loved the Lord.

When his own failings threatened to destroy him, David found his footing on the rock. Like the woman who washed Jesus's feet with her long hair, like the young disciple John who leaned against Jesus at the Last Supper, David responded to the Lord by loving him.

Psalm 18 repeats the song that is found in 2 Samuel and adds these words: "I love you, O Lord, my strength…"

David sang it, and because it is in the book of Psalm, probably everyone else did too.

Centuries later, the humble fisherman, Peter, would have known this psalm. He probably sang it.

When Peter said, "You are the Christ, the Son of the Living God," and Jesus replied, "On this Rock, I will build my church," Peter recognized the rock he meant.

This rock is somehow personal. "We find in him joy and rescue and help. He is interested in us! In me! He delights in us (in me), and we (I) can relax and delight in him!"

David uses the personal voice here. He speaks not for a nation (though he could have as king). He speaks for himself, a man who has been in terrible sin and in terrible danger and has found himself brought through, not by time and circumstance, but by the one he calls his rock, his fortress, and his deliverer.

Do we see Jesus here? Is it stretching it? Remember, "all the fullness of God's glory was found in him (Jesus)."

Find an area in which you have conflict with someone. Call on God, your rock, your fortress, and the underlying meaning of your experience.

Find an area where you have a weakness. Ask God to be your rock. Acknowledge that he is.

What difference does this make?

Think of something that is out of control. Jesus is the rock. Bring this situation to him.

CHAPTER 5

Other Psalms and Other Singers

The warm rain fell in the broad Sacramento valley, and fell and fell. It filled the reservoirs and pushed the rivers out of the banks. It fell in the mountains and melted the snow, and the runoff was alarming. In just a few days, we were in the grip of a hundred-year flood.

Outside Marysville, a couple visiting from New Jersey (where they think they have bad weather) got in their car and started out for higher land. In the darkness, they took a wrong turn and found themselves stuck on a deserted road as the water rose around them. It wasn't flowing fast, but it kept rising until there was no place to go but the top of their car They stood there, clinging to each other, in waist-high water for eighteen hours It must have felt like the experience of David.

> The cords of death encompassed
> me, the torrents of perdition assailed
> me. (Psalm 18.4)

Finally, they were spotted by a helicopter crew and rescued! Their friend, following in the darkness, was lost in the flood They survived because they were standing on something high enough and something firm

Psalm 18 (and 2 Samuel 22) is a song about an experience like this. It is intense and personal. We know it came from David's heart at a time of crisis. He had been fighting men bigger and better equipped than his men (a man of great size, with six fingers on each hand and six toes on each foot), and enemy equipped with new weapons. David grew weary, but God gave the victory, and on the day he was delivered from all his enemies, David sang this song.

There is a score of references to "the rock" in the Psalm—some written by David, some by others, and much of the time, the author is unknown It doesn't matter! These are songs that belong to everyone, and the Israelites sang them, and so do we. These songs are the very weapons of our warfare! This is music to remind us that we have a great resource and a great promise and that we have a God who puts hope in our hearts in every situation.

Some of the psalms have been reworked in the idiom of modern songwriters. We sing, "Rock of

Ages, cleft for me, let me hide myself in thee," and we sing the meaning of Psalm 25.5, which says "In the day of trouble, he will keep me safe in his dwelling. He will hide me in the shelter of his tabernacle and set me high on a rock."

When we sing, "When my heart is overcome, then lead me to the rock, the rock that is higher, higher than I," we are singing the words of the Psalm 61.

A lot of these psalms are about protection—the rock as a fortress and a dependable place to stand. In addition to Psalm 27, these are some of the psalms that call on the Lord, the rock, for help:

Psalm 28:1 NIV   "To you I call, O Lord, my Rock."

Psalm 31:3 NIV   "Come quickly to my rescue; be my rock of refuge, a strong fortress to save me."

Psalm 40:2 NIV   "He lifted me out of the slimy pit, out of the mud and mire, he set my foot on a rock and gave me a firm place to stand."

Psalm 62:2 NIV   "He alone is my rock and my salvation; he is my fortress, I will never be shaken."

Psalm 71:3 NIV   "Be my rock of refuge, to which I can always go; give the command to save me, for you are my rock and my fortress."

Psalm 94:22 NIV "The Lord is become my fortress, and my God the rock in whom I take refuge."

Other psalms sing about the rock in the wilderness from which the water sprang. These are songs of praise and thankfulness. They celebrate the Lord who does marvelous and amazing things and does so to care for his people. "The Lord takes thought for *me*" (Psalm 40:17) is one of the most amazing things of all!

Here are a couple of "water from the rock" psalms:

Psalm 105: 41 "He opened the rock and water gushed out; it flowed through the desert like a river."

Psalm 114:8 NIV "Tremble O Earth, at the presence of the Lord, who turns the rock into a pool of water, the flint into a spring of water."

So long ago, the Israelites sang about their god-lit history. Did they ponder the theology of this image? Probably not any more than we normally do. But it went deep into attitude and expectation. It was part of the way they approached God, and so it can be for us—a song in the heart as we approach our King.

CHAPTER 6

Daniel and the Rock

There is a God in heaven who reveals mysteries.
—Daniel 2:28 NIV

"A stone was cut out, not by human hands
and it struck the statue on its' feet of iron
and clay and broke them into pieces. But the
stone that struck the statue became a great
mountain and filled the whole earth."
—Daniel 2:34–35 NIV

Daniel in Babylon is the story of a good Jewish boy in the court of a hostile Middle Eastern dictator. Long before the days of Islam, the Babylonian empire was the most powerful force in the world (as they knew it). It was a power center of wealth, culture, and military might. Babylonians invaded Israel, and the country, weakened by poor kings and careless people, fell easily. The Babylonians took captives the youngest and strongest and best educated. These young Hebrew men and women would live out their years in a hostile culture as slaves.

Because the Babylonian captors recognized their superior education, understanding, and competence, Daniel and several other young men were taken into the service of the king. They were to be trained in Chaldean literature and language. It was to be a Babylonian brain trust. They were treated like royalty, but they were surrounded by enemies of Israel.

The first chapter of Daniel sets the stage. The man who will become a rare kind of hero is first a young boy, far from home, and beset by pressures he can hardly be expected to resist. But resist them he does, and this flint in his character makes the rest of the drama possible. Take time to read the whole book; it's only twelve chapters long, and it's full of amazement.

Some Middle Eastern nations have been in conflict with the United States and other Western countries for some time. But the United States is big and powerful, and these countries, while often dangerous, are a lot smaller and less sophisticated in the ways of war. But imagine if they were large and much more powerful, and imagine the US was as small as, say, New Jersey. Now imagine, there has been a conquest, and the best and the brightest young people from Stanford, Harvard, and the University of Chicago have been taken to the Middle

East, where they will spend their lives in service to an enemy government.

This is close to the situation in which David found himself. Israel had been a nation for about four hundred years. Babylon was the great and stable world power. It far overshadowed little Israel in commerce and world affairs, and for a time, it ruled over it.

This is the same part of the world where Islam would later flourish. The Babylonians of that time worshipped Moloch—an idol that they thought brought them power and prosperity in exchange for blood of animals and children.

The Israelites never made their home in Babylonia as they had in Egypt. They were temporary residents, captives. They were never in danger of taking Babylonian gods as their own. But the Babylonian empire was enormous. It had superior weaponry and tremendous world influence. From a human point of view, power lay securely in the courts of Babylon.

The Babylonians laid siege to Jerusalem and succeeded in conquering it twice. They took away sacred objects from the temple, and they took young men from the royal families and made them slaves or possibly eunuchs. These young men were bright and well educated. The Babylonians added their own training and used these men to run the country; they were second-level administrators.

Daniel was one of these.

The king was having nightmares. When Daniel went to tell the king what his dream was, he said what the palace wise men had said, with one variation. He said, "No one can show to the king the mystery that the king is asking, but there is a God in heaven who reveals mysteries, and he has shown the king what will happen at the end of days."

There is good news and bad news here. The dream was a serious concern; it was a true vision of the future, and it came from God.

Daniel said to him, "To you, O, King, as you lay in bed, came thoughts of what would be hereafter, and the revealer of mysteries disclosed to you what is to be."

Daniel refers to "the revealer of mysteries" and "the God of heaven" and "the ancient of days" when he speaks the Lord. He is using terminology that is both accurate and accessible to a Babylonian.

Daniel described a statue ninety feet tall, made of strata of material. On top, there is gold, followed by silver, bronze, iron, and finally, at the feet, clay. It represented the Babylonian Empire, and its decline.

(Daniel, who had saved them all from limb from limb with his revelations, was probably risking the same fate all over again by presenting such a woeful view of the years to come.)

This is where it gets interesting. Daniel told the king that he, Nebuchadnezzar, had seen a stone cut, "not by human hands, and it struck the statue on its feet of iron and clay and broke them into pieces," and the whole statue, the whole nation, crumbled and blew away. "But the stone that struck the statue became a great mountain, and it filled the whole earth."

Daniel makes it clear: after the destruction of these kingdoms, the God of heaven will set up a kingdom that shall never be destroyed…it will endure forever.

You don't have to be a student of Middle Eastern history to see what this means. The Babylonians were masters of their part of the world, but their kingdom would be crushed and "the wind will blow it away without a trace."

Then the great Babylonian King did what few powerful men have done. He fell on his face, saying, "Surely your God is God of gods and Lord of lords and a revealer of mysteries."

There is something intriguing about the Babylonians. Even though they were cruel despots and worshipped a false god, from time to time, the God of Israel spoke to them. And sometimes, they listened.

Now, the matter of the dreams. In the second year of his reign, the Babylonian King Nebuchadnezzar had such disturbing dreams that he couldn't sleep at night. He called the palace magicians, wise men, and the Chaldeans (who were not from Chaldea but rather a higher order of wise men). He insisted that first they tell him the dream and *then* tell him the meaning of it. In today's terminology, we would say the king was obsessed with the dreams and with what they meant.

The wise men argued that no one could tell what the king dreamed "except the gods, whose dwelling is not with mortals." At this, the king "flew into a violent rage and issued a decree that all the wise men be executed."

Daniel and the three men who had come with him were included in this group, even though they were very young, and they were foreigners. Daniel asked for time, and he would tell the king what the dream was (evidently, it was one recurring dream) and what it meant. Daniel went home and asked his friends to pray—to "seek mercy from the God of heaven."

God revealed the mystery to Daniel in a vision of the night, and before he went to see the king, Daniel gave thanks and praise to God.

Let's talk about this for a moment. Daniel was living in the great Babylonian civilization, which was famous for its wisdom and power, but that wisdom had failed. Daniel saw that power and wisdom lay with the God of his ancestors, and he praised him for it.

> "Blessed be the name of God from
>   Age to age,
> for wisdom and power are his.
> He reveals deep and hidden things;
> he knows what is in the darkness.

and light dwells with him." (Daniel
2:20–22 NIV)

The words the king uses, the very non-Hebrew words, are important. He was recognizing God as he could discern him, not the shepherd of Israel and not the God of Jacob for those promises were not made to him. Later, Daniel would use the names the God of heaven and ancient of days—names that showed that God was not limited to Israel or the descendants of Abraham.

King Nebuchadnezzar saw God as greater than the gods of Babylon and as Lord of the spiritual powers that Babylon knew. He saw what Daniel saw—the God of wisdom and power, the one who "knows what is in the darkness," and "the revealer of mysteries." Yahweh, the Hebrew God, had shown the king, in his dream, reality. He could not have understood it in the normal human course of things.

Far from the Promised Land, in cruel Babylon, the good news is heard:

> There is a God in Heaven who
> reveals mysteries, and he has dis-
> closed to Kind Nebuchadnezzar
> what will happen at the end of days.

So God, the God of heaven (not a localized deity) made himself known to the King of Persia! The dream told of the end of one of the world's great civilizations. It was struck by a stone not cut by human hands. And the stone which struck the statue became a great mountain and filled the whole earth.

This is apocalyptic writing, a writing meant to uncover or reveal something. Don't try to fit it into too many holes. Just remember it.

Task:

God revealed himself to an outsider, Daniel's God is the God of heaven. Look for God at work in someone outside the family of faith. Pray for someone in the news.

Blessing:

May the God of all nations bless our nation today. May he use you and me to bring his love to the community where we live out our daily lives.

Daniel and the Rock

Read Daniel 2:1–16.

1. Describe Daniel's situation.
2. Compare Daniel's demeanor with that of Nebuchadnezzar. Which man had the most power?

3. In verses 17–23, describe what Daniel did. Where did he get support? What did he tell the king about his God?
4. In verses 24–30, suddenly, there was a lot of hustling about. Describe what happened next. Who was involved?
5. In verses 31–35, David told the king his dream, and he told it in detail.
6. Verses 36–45 talks about the interpretation of the dream. What did Daniel say about the king? And about where his power came from? What did he say about the kingdom that the God of heaven would set up? What did he say about the stone? Contrast the god of the Babylonians and the God of Daniel. What do you think the point of this story is?

JESUS IS THE ROCK

Second Six-Week Session

Week 7 Isaiah 8:14, 17:10, 32:2 NIV Romans 9:23 NIV Isaiah 26:16 NIV Jeremiah 2:12–13 NIV	The Trouble with a Rock…A Rock of Stumbling Living by faith is not an option—either we trust God, or we don't.
Week 8 John 7:37–39 NIV Jeremiah 2:12–13 NIV	Anyone Who Is Thirsty

Week 9

On This Rock—A Rock
to Build a Life On
Matthew 16:13–18,
7:24, 21:42, 27:60 NIV
Acts 4:11 NIV
Luke 6:48, 8:6 NIV
Ephesians 2:20 NIV
1 Peter 2:6 NIV
Isaiah 28:16 NIV—"A
stone in Zion"

Week 10

The Rock as a
Hiding Place
Romans 9:30–32 NIV,
Isaiah 22:16 NIV

Week 11

The Invitation…The
Rock—Petra or Petros
1 Peter 2:4f NIV, 1
Peter 2:49 NIV
Psalm 62:6 NIV—"He
alone is my rock."
Psalm 61:2 NIV—"Lead
me to the rock that
is higher than I."

Week 12   Jesus All Along…Jesus
                 Is the Cornerstone
                 1 Corinthians 10:1–4,
                 15:4–8, 3:11 NIV
                 Matthew 21:42 NIV
                 Ephesians 2:20 NIV
                 Acts 4:11 NIV
                 1 Peter 2:6 NIV
                 1 Timothy 6:19 NIV
Week 13   The Voice at the
                 End of the World…A
                 Rock of Destiny
                 1 Peter 2:8 NIV
                 Romans 9:33 NIV
                 Revelation 21:5–6 NIV

Summary comments
What I have learned in this study and my personal
comments

CHAPTER 7

The Trouble with a Rock

And he will be a sanctuary, but for both
houses of Israel, he will be a stone that
causes men to stumble and a rock that
makes them fall. And for the people of
Jerusalem he will be a trap and a snare.
—Isaiah 8:14 NIV

You have forgotten God, your Savior. You have
not remembered the Rock, your fortress.
—Isaiah 17:10 NIV

Trust in the Lord forever, for the Lord,
the Lord, is the Rock eternal.
—Isaiah 26:4 NIV

Thus says the Lord God,
"See, I am laying in Zion a foundation stone,
a tested stone,
a precious cornerstone, a sure foundation:

> One who trusts will not panic.
> And I will make justice the line,
> and righteousness the plummet."
> —Isaiah 28:16 NIV

> Be appalled, O heavens, at this,
> be shocked, be utterly desolate, says the Lord,
> for my people have committed two evils:
> they have forsaken me,
> the fountain of living water,
> and dug out cisterns for themselves,
> cracked cisterns, that can hold no water.
> —Jeremiah 2:12–13

The major prophets wanted to talk about "the rock." And the people probably didn't want to hear. The problem with a rock is this: you can't do much to it. If it is a really big rock, an escarpment, a field of granite, or the mantle of the earth, you can't do anything at all except trip over it or build on it.

Isaiah the prophet lived about seven hundred years before the time of Christ. (There were probably two writers of Isaiah. It is only the first we are concerned with here.)

The nation of Israel, conceived in freedom and in faithfulness to Jehovah, had faltered. The temptation to live as their neighbors lived proved too compelling to resist. Instead of looking to God, they trusted in human plans and resources. The system of priests as rulers had given way to kings, some of whom trusted in the Lord, and some who trusted only in themselves.

By Isaiah's time, there was a problem. The appearance of power was this: Israel had divided into two kingdoms. The northern kingdom had been annexed to Assyria. The southern kingdom, Judah, lived in fragile independence on the borders of a powerful and aggressive neighbor. These were hard times for God's people. It didn't look like the Promised Land anymore.

But the reality was still there. Israel belonged to God. God loved Israel and all her people. He was still the bedrock on which they existed.

Isaiah reminds them of this:

> Do not call conspiracy all that this people calls conspiracy, and do not fear what it fears, or be in dread. But the Lord of hosts, him you shall regard as holy. Let him be your fear and let him be your dread. (Isaiah 8:12 NIV)

For Israel, the reality was different than the appearance of reality. God was still a personal God, and he was still involved. Isaiah had more to say: "He will become a sanctuary, a stone one strikes against; for both houses of Israel he will become a rock one stumbles over."

You can't ignore a rock—not if it's massive and not if it's right there in your backyard, underfoot, so to speak.

This is what happened to Israel. The Israelites were God's people, his chosen. They knew he was supposed to be the underlying reality of their lives. But they honored the heroes of the faith without honoring the God these men and women knew. Some trusted only in themselves. Some put their hope in political strategies. Some dabbled in the religions of the tribes around them. The worship of Baal, the god of power and conquest, and the worship of Ashteroth, the goddess of sexuality and fertility, became common. The Israelites were no longer faithful. The love that David had for the Lord was not found in these people.

But the Lord was still present, and he became the rock that made them fall. They were tripped by their own unfaithfulness.

But he would also become a "sanctuary," a place of holiness and safety. How can these two ideas, these side-by-side prophecies both be true? We have a good picture of this in our own time.

Across the Midwest, summer conditions of heat and air pressure cook up tornadoes. In countless backyards, a wedge of concrete with a sturdy door attached juts up just above the grass in the back-yard, a nuisance and a hazard—something to trip over. But on that day, when the sky darkens and an ominous funnel appears, blowing over the open countryside, it is a welcome refuge!

Being in reach of a storm cellar can mean the difference between life and death. It is both a place to stumble and a place to find safety.

In fact, these are the words that Jesus quoted in talking with the Pharisees. He explained them, "The kingdom of God will be taken away from you and given to a people who produces the fruits of it" (Matthew 21:42–44).

It is inescapable. "The one who falls on that stone will be broken to pieces; and it will crush anyone on whom it falls."

Hidden in the chapters of Isaiah is the link of prophecy. In the next chapter, in the sixth verse, we come upon a wonderful vision—a vision that was not to become a reality for another seven hundred years!

> For a child has been born to us, a
>   son given to us;
> authority rests on his shoulders and
>   he is named
> Wonderful Counselor, Mighty God,
> Everlasting Father, Prince of Peace.
>   (Isaiah 9:6 NIV)

But it is Jeremiah who has the last sad word on this subject. It is another generation. The Israelites were, by this time, in exile in Babylon. Jeremiah, the prophet, accompanied them there, and he spoke God's words to them, both a comfort and rebuke:

> Be appalled, O heavens, at this,
> be shocked, be utterly desolate…
> for my people have committed two
>   evils:
> they have forsaken me,
> the fountain of living water
> and dug out cisterns for themselves,
> crooked cisterns that can hold no
>   water. (Jeremiah 2:12 NIV)

What a contrast! Living water from the living rock. It burst onto the dry desert floor, God's good gift. Every minimally observant Hebrew knew this story.

But Israel wasn't trusting God who gave the water. Jeremiah laments:

> "What wrong did your ancestors find
>   in me?"
> asks the Lord in the prophet's voice,
> "That they went far from me
> and went after worthless things
> and became worthless themselves."
> (Jeremiah 2:5)

This is exactly what Israel had done. It was a time of ungodly leadership and unfaithful followers. Issues of justice and mercy were put aside as leaders devised plans and strategies for survival with the Assyrians.

They had reduced the worship of the living God to a set of ceremonies. It had nothing to do with issues of justice and mercy and trust. The character and soul of the people was starved and diminished.

In a semiarid land, it was common practice to bury large clay pots in the ground, where water could be stored. But these pots were fragile. They could easily crack even after they were buried, and then every bit of precious water would drain into the ground. It was the practical thing to do—practical until the inevitable cracks developed.

What does this sad story have to do with the good news of Jesus Christ? Everything!

Living by faith was never an option. Either we trust God, or we don't. Either we wait for the living water in the wilderness, or we build a system of safeguards for ourselves, guarantees for the future, and cisterns that we hope won't crack.

How easy it is to rely on every modern resource and forget the fountain of living water. It is the difference between doing things to earn our place with God and living by faith by asking and receiving.

The alternative to relying on uncertain earthly resources is trusting God—always a risky business and not easy to defend to a clamoring family or a cynical neighbor. But it also means risking miracles and deliverance. With a cistern, you only risk the cracks.

Task:

Watch for the "leaky cisterns" in your life, the places where you count on your own resources. They may be in the area of finances or reputation or education. They may be in areas of relationships. Trade them in for God's ongoing care and provision. It's a question of whom you really trust!

Take one of the verses from the beginning of this chapter. Memorize it. Claim it as your own.

Blessing:

May the God of eternal security be present and known to you as earthly things reveal their transience. May you take encouragement in the reality of his love and care.

CHAPTER 8

Anyone Who Is Thirsty

On the last day of the festival, the great day,
while Jesus was standing there, he cried
out, "Let anyone who is thirsty come to me
and let the one who believes in me drink
As the scripture has said, 'Out of the believer's
heart shall flow rivers of living water.'"
Now he said this about the Spirit, which the
believers were to receive; for as yet there was not
the Spirit, because Jesus was not yet glorified.
—John 7:37–39 NIV

Why is this passage important in a study such as
this? There is no mention of a rock here. The answer
lies in what was going on as Jesus spoke.

It was the last day of the Festival of Tabernacles,
the holiday celebrating the time in the wilderness.
Jesus was in Jerusalem at the end of his earthly
ministry. For three years, he had been walking the
roads of Israel, preaching in the marketplaces, and

teaching on the hillsides. He had healed and taught and talked with people long enough so that all the right questions were being asked. People watched him—people who were steeped in the concept of one God, holy, and all mighty.

These people knew the Shema, "Hear O Israel, the Lord your God is One God." They sang the psalms, "Blessed be my Rock and may the God of my salvation be exalted."

No Jew entertained a visual image of God. The Commandments expressly forbade the religious use of images, whether in the form of a statue, a standing stone, or any other *thing.* They understood that the picture of a rock or a fountain gushing water was just that—a picture. The idea of God beyond human imagination was well established.

But Jesus stood before them and said (shouted),"Let anyone who is thirsty, come to *me.*" And he said, "Out of the believer's heart shall flow rivers of living water."

Jesus did not claim to *have* the spirit of God; he claimed to *give* it!

For some, it was a shift in the way the world was put together. For others who had been waiting, it fit. It was the "Aha!" or even the "at last!"

We are different from first-century Jews; they had an immediate context in which to understand these words and actions. Ours is distant and limited by ignorance.

An immediate political consequence hung over their heads if they responded to Jesus. We who live in Western countries don't fear that, but they had to gather enough information to make a response, and in that way, we are the same. They had to come down on one side or the other, and so do we. For some of us, it's easy, a glad relief, a welcome home. For some, it's a leap into belief.

Now, a word about how we handle meaning. Kenneth Bailey, in his wonderful book *Finding the Lost*, draws on a lifetime of living in the Middle East to point out that "the Western mind has done its serious thinking in concepts." We are interested in the *idea*, and we use story and metaphor to illuminate it.

The Middle Easterner constructs meaning with the story, the metaphor, the proverb. This may be explained and commented on, but the commentary is secondary. It is the story which counts.

Dr. Bailey puts it very carefully. He says, "The person involved is not illustrating a concept but rather creating meaning by reference to something concrete."

No one in Israel seemed to be in danger of worshipping a rock or even venerating one. (That would later be done in Mecca, where a great black stone, supposedly given to Abraham by the angel Gabriel, is enshrined.)

Jesus spoke a great reality. It was much more than a story, much more than an idea. He was and he is the rock, the great underlying reality upon which all of creation rests, out of whom all of life flows.

On that great day, in a public square in Jerusalem, in that man Jesus, all of this came together.

There is another facet to this story. Jesus stood by the pool of Siloam. During the seven days of the Feast of Tabernacles (or Tents), it was the custom to bring water from that pool to the temple. The priest brought it in a golden pitcher, a reminder of the time in the wilderness and the water from the rock; a reminder also that Messiah would someday come.

Jesus stood with the crowd around him and claimed that identity. "Let anyone who is thirsty come to me!" he shouted so that everyone around him could hear.

He quoted scripture they all knew: "Out of the believer's heart will flow rivers of living water."

He spoke about the Holy Spirit, who was yet to come. (The word we translate as "heart" is really "belly"—out of his gut, from deep inside, will flow living water.)

It's all one piece. Messiah, the Holy One of Israel, had been there all along in the wilderness. And the rock was only a glimpse of the one who could quench the longing of the human soul. Any Jewish man and any Jewish woman standing there would know that Jesus of Nazareth claimed to be that one.

The prophecy of Joel is also in the air:

"I will pour out my spirit upon all flesh. Your sons and daughters shall prophesy, your old men shall dream dreams, your young men will see visions. I will pour out my Spirit." (Joel 2:28 NIV)

The story is greater than the idea, and the reality is greater than the story. The cry "Come to me anyone who thirsts" is an invitation to live. All the twists of history and human machinations are lost in the moment of real meeting. No wonder the Pharisees panicked!

Tasks:

How does the human thirst for God—your own thirst and that of someone close to you—show itself?

How is it hidden or disguised?

What does it mean to come to Jesus? What are some of the consequences?

What are the effects of *not* responding to Jesus's invitation?

Blessing:

May you relax and come and may that promised Holy Spirit satisfy your deepest need.

CHAPTER 9

ON THIS ROCK I WILL BUILD MY CHURCH

"Who do people say the Son of Man is?"
And they said, "Some say John the
Baptist and others Elijah and still other
Jerimiah or one of the prophets."
He said to them, "But who do you say that I am?"
Simon Peter answered, "You are the
Messiah, the Son of the Living God."
And Jesus answered him saying, "Blessed
are you, Simon son of Jonah, for flesh and
blood has not revealed this to you, but my
Father in heaven and I tell you, you are Peter
and on this rock I will build my church."
—Matthew 16:13–18 NIV

If you are going to be crossing San Francisco Bay
when an earthquake hits, the bridge to be on is the
Golden Gate. Suspended high in the foggy air and
above treacherous tides, it is the safest bridge in the
bay area. Engineers worry about the Oakland Bay

Bridge and the Richmond, both long, low spans, whose support is set in soil that quivers like a bowl of chocolate pudding when a tremor ripples through. In fact, during the Loma Prieta earthquake of 1989, a section of the Oakland Bay Bridge did fail, and a motorist tipped over the opened section of bridge and died.

But the span of the Golden Gate is hung from towers set into rock. The pulse of the earthquake, which builds and reverberates with the looser soil of the other bridges, hits the rock and nothing moves.

There have been signs all along that Jesus is the Messiah, the "anointed one." The first time that Andrew saw Jesus in the days when John was baptizing in the Jordan, he ran and told his brother Simon that they had found the Messiah (John 1:35–42).

Later, Jesus would attack the religious officials of the time, the Pharisees and Sadducees, for letting their own self-importance obscure the signals God was giving, and so they failed to understand what was going on. First, they demanded signs, and then they failed to notice them.

Finally, Jesus said that there would be only one sign, the sign of Jonah—the man who was swallowed by death and after three days in the belly of the fish, came into the land of the living again.

His own followers disappointed him when they failed to understand his meaning when he told them to beware of this "yeast of the Pharisees." They thought he was talking about dinner.

"How could you fail to perceive that I was not speaking about bread?" he railed at them. He had given them enough clues.

Jesus speaks openly now to the foundation of faith.

All three synoptic gospels record this conversation. Unlike many of the other stories, there is almost no variation and no differing point of view. Everyone who was there remembered it exactly.

One day, alone with is disciples, Jesus put the question to them. "Who do men say that I am?"

They had plenty of time to figure it out, but they answered him with all the gossip that was going around the streets and marketplaces of Judea.

"The people think you are John the Baptist, raised from the dead."

"Or maybe Elijah."

"They say you are a prophet."

"Maybe Jeremiah," all the answers of all the other people.

And then Jesus turns to Peter, "But you…who do *you* say that I am?"

Was there hesitation then?

The answer would push across the line into idolatry or a whole new way of looking at the world.

Peter said what the others did not dare, what had been in the air since Jesus first called his disciples, and what Andrew suspected he might be the "chosen one."

"You are the Messiah, the Christ, the Son of the Living God."

And with that, we have come at last to the bottom line.

Jesus is the Rock, the underlying reality of Jewish experience, and indeed, of all creation, the great truth of all existence.

The cleft in the rock where one may stand to see the Holy One pass by, the One who followed and led in a pillar of cloud and fire, the God who was "among his people like a king," whom Balaam saw and who was in David's song and in Daniel's vision.

Jesus of Nazareth is the Messiah, the Christ, the God who became man, the Emmanuel.

In those moments, the world shifts, and its true form is seen. The divine invitation is met with the human "yes!" and the church is born.

All the false starts, the misunderstandings are past, and all phony gods are deflated. The disciples have entered the new life, forever in harmony with God and permanently *out* of harmony with this passing world.

It is no coincidence that at this point, Jesus began to prepare them for his suffering and death. And for the disciples as well, the battle with their own world was engaged. They would be ignored, discounted, and finally persecuted openly. Most of them would be killed. The sides were chosen, and the death throes of the enemy would be deadly.

Task:

Here is the only task that counts: 'Who do *you* say that I am?"

Blessing:

May you recognize the new life you live in Christ. May you know the old gods are dust. May you praise God in the midst of opposition.

CHAPTER 10

The Rock as a Hiding Place

What then are we to say? Gentiles, who did not
strive for righteousness, have a attained it, that
is righteousness through faith; but Israel, who
did strive for righteousness that is based on the
law, did not succeed in fulfilling that law. Why
not? Because they did not strive for it based on
faith, but as if it were based on works. They have
stumbled over the stumbling stone, as it is written:
"See, I am laying in Zion a stone
that will make people stumble.
A rock that will make them fall, and whoever
believes in him, will not be put to shame."
—Romans 9:30–33 NIV

What are we to say about the fairness of God? Why
are not all the descendants of Abraham, that chosen
family, automatically saved? What about Isaac and
all of his offspring? Why do so many Gentiles, outsiders who were never part of the original promises,

step into new life in Christ with hardly a struggle? It doesn't seem fair. It's not! The whole story of God's dealings with humankind is not about fairness; it's about mercy…and the sovereign love of God. God acts because he chooses to act. He loves because he chooses to love!

These words of Paul to the Romans were written in great frustration because of his personal journey as a Pharisee, a lawyer of the scripture, and a zealot who persecuted the Christians. Why did outsiders inherit what God's chosen could not seem to grasp? Why did they inherit when they weren't even trying? The children of Israel stumbled over the foundation stone; they pursued the righteousness of God with their own good works. They would not take the gift but insisted on earning it, on working the system, and on doing it themselves.

Hosea, the prophet of Israel's unfaithful years, pours out God's grieving love:

> "Yet the Israelites will be like the sand on the seashore, which cannot be measured or counted. In the place where it was said to them. 'You are not my people,' they will be called 'sons of the living God.' The people of Judah and the people of Israel will be reunited, and they will appoint one leader and will come up out of the land, for great will be the day of

Jezreel (son of Hosea and Gomer,
the adulterous wife)." (Hosea 1:10–11
NIV)

The stone was laid up in Zion by a loving God. The attention of the Holy One and the law, was given to the nation of Israel. It was there for the taking, but it was there in the person of Jesus, the Messiah, the righteous one, and the one who came to fulfill the law.

Crossing Kansas in a motor home in the heat of summer can be a threatening experience. The clouds piled up in the eastern sky, and though it was the middle of the afternoon, a wall of darkness enveloped our vision. The air was still and hot.

The radio crackled with weather advisories; electrical storm cells formed across the northern half of the state. We pulled off the interstate and waited it out under an overpass. It offered some protection when the wind velocity frightened us. Lightning split the sky with one deafening crack after another. We were in the middle of it. A tornado hit a town we had driven through an hour back down the road. The damage, we heard later, was small, one house and a couple of sheds demolished, a truck turned over, and two cows killed. A family lived in the house, and they were all at home. It was a rented house, and in the backyard, a heavy steel door jutted out of the grassy lawn.

"I hated that thing," the wife said, when they interviewed her on the evening news. "It spoiled the look of the yard, and we were always running into it in the dark." But that day, they pulled the door open, and the family and two dogs and a cat hid in the safety of that storm cellar while a tornado churned across the grass and reduced the house to splinters. There was no other place to be safe. This is the kind of shelter God offers us in the rock—when there is no other place to be safe.

The Apostle Paul speaks to this. He quotes the prophet Isaiah.

> "See, I am laying in Zion a foundation stone, a tested stone, a precious corner stone, a sure foundation. One who trusts in him will not panic." (Isaiah 28:16 NIV)

And yes, justice and righteousness is part of it. Isaiah uses the builder's tools to make the point. "I will make justice the line…and righteousness the plummet."

Much of the book of Romans talks about the great inheritance of the Jews and the miracle that has been offered to the whole of humankind. In Romans, as in Daniel and Isaiah, we get the idea that God's glory and care is for everyone. All nations and people belong to him. All the naysayers and cynics may say yes. All the outsiders may come in.

God provides a shelter—his Son, the *rock*—in the time of trouble…all for our salvation.

Some Questions:

1. In what ways do people stumble over this rock?
2. Do we/I ever resent his being in the path of our/my daily routines?
3. Read over Romans 9. Given Paul's assurance in 8:39, why did he now discuss the problem of widespread Jewish unbelief? How did he account for their unbelief in spite of such advantages (vv. 6–9; also 4:11–12)?
4. How deeply do you hurt for unbelievers? Why?
5. Have you ever wondered why God chose you to be part of his plan for the universe?
6. In what area are you growing in your understanding of God's will for your life?
7. How do you interpret Isiah 8:14 and 28:16 for your own life?

Task:

There is none! He, the rock, has done it all. His sacrifice is your salvation.

Blessing:

"Peace be to the whole community and love, with faith, from God the Father and the Lord Jesus Christ." (The blessing from the end of the letter to the Ephesians.)

CHAPTER 11

THE FOUNDATION INVITATION

Come to him, a living stone, though rejected by
mortals yet chosen and precious in God's sight.
—1 Peter 2:4 NIV

How far does the rock beneath the topsoil, the bedrock, extend? If you could dig deeply enough, you would find that it extends over the whole earth! Beneath the sand and soil of the whole world and beneath all ocean beds lies a layer of dense rock, the mantle of the earth.

In some places, such as the great mountain ranges, it is right up on top where it can be seen. In the Sierra, for instance, great domes of granite glisten in the sun, and the sparse trees have to put down roots in whatever soil is caught in crack or crevice.

In other places, the bedrock is buried beneath ages of silty deposits. You can farm in places like this, but beware of bridges there and tall buildings.

Mexico City is built in such a place, and when the earthquake of 1985 struck, the soft sediment quivered like jelly. More than eight thousand people died and thirty thousand were injured. Not everyone was injured by the jolting of the earthquake itself; far more treacherous were the buildings that tilted and collapsed when the soil beneath them failed. There is no rock for the foundations there.

A "rock" is just a metaphor, an image to help us think about the real thing in an accurate and meaningful way. It is not a good idea to push it beyond its intended use. But sometimes, it's hard to resist doing just that!

Look at Jesus's words in the Gospel of Luke, "Why do you call me Lord, Lord and do not do what I tell you? I will tell you what someone is like who comes to me, hears my words and acts on them. That one is like a man building a house, who dug deeply and laid the foundation on rock. That house will stand."

So what do words have to do with it?

Jesus asked the critical question, "Who do you say that I am?"

It was a face-to-face question, and Peter had enough knowledge to give the answer. It was a confession and a commitment.

"You are the Christ, the son of the Living God!"

The priests and the Sadducees probably had as much information as Peter had, but it was left to Peter, a very ordinary working man, to say the words that acknowledged the King of kings. These are words that count, words that brought from Jesus the response, "On this rock I will build my church."

A generation later, Peter, now an aged believer, experienced in trust and persecution, wrote to believers in Asia Minor. He was encouraging them with the truth of the path they had taken and the amazing truth that would always be out of compliance with the appearance of reality around them.

He wrote:

> Come to him, to Christ, the living stone!
> And like living stones, let yourselves be built into a spiritual house, to be a holy priesthood, offering spiritual sacrifices acceptable to God through Jesus Christ. (1 Peter 2:4–5 NIV)

No believer will become a fossil, locked in the dead and unchanging past, a relic of some outdated idea. That is the lie the world offers. Jesus is the living rock, an artesian spring which produces living water. We are part of that, as fresh and living as an artesian spring, formed along a shelf of underground rock.

Peter was talking about this living stone which was also the foundation of faith.

He quotes in Isaiah 28:16 NIV:

"See, I am laying in Zion a stone,
a cornerstone, chosen and precious,
and whoever believes in him will not
be put to shame."

It is a reference to the rock—the underlying, unchanging nature of God—and to the deep schism that arose as soon as Jesus was identified with that rock.

To you then who believe, he is precious, but for those who do not
believe,
"The stone that the builders rejected,
has become the very head of the
corner,"
and
"A stone that makes them stumble
and a rock that makes them fall."
(Psalm 118:22)

Wow! It's a lot to digest, yet it's very simple: Jesus is the living rock, the underlying reality of existence. Jesus is God!

It's no surprise that this may seem unreal at times. It goes against what most of the world says is reasonable. After all, Jesus has been diminished and disbelieved for centuries. It's no wonder there is some confusion. It is confusion set in our paths by the enemy.

Still, the reality remains. At the point we meet our own unbelief, we have a chance to experience this exact reality. It is a choice. As we come to him, we find our true selves. We become God's own.

A woman was asked if she really believed everything in the Bible. She thought for a moment. Her questioner was someone she loved and respected.

"Well," she said, "I don't always believe it. I'm enough a child of my time to have doubts. But nevertheless, I keep experiencing it—the truth of the gospel, the goodness of God."

It's an honest answer, the answer of a believer in a cynical age.

It's unlikely that the exiles in Asia Minor felt like part of anything the world called important. These people were primarily the outsiders and the underprivileged. They were migrant workers (resident aliens), slaves, and wives of unbelieving husbands. They were not conforming to the expectations of their employers, their owners, or their households But they belong to Jesus, and so they are his forever—something very special.

But Peter, the fisherman and the apostle, told them:

> You are a chosen race, a royal priesthood a holy nation, God's own people, in order that you may proclaim the mighty acts of him who

called you out of darkness into his marvelous light!"

All the clues have been given. The great mystery is revealed. There is a wonderful sense of resolution, of resolution, in this passage. We know now what God has been doing all along. And we know that we are included and meant to be part of what God is building. We may expect to find ourselves in deadly conflict with a world, determined to ignore this reality.

But the truth is Jesus is the rock. He is the one who will save or cause the downfall of a man or a woman or a nation. He is the one who has always been there, the underlying reality and the cause of creation. He calls us "out of darkness into his marvelous light."

Task:

John Muir wrote that no true invitation is ever declined. And this is the most compelling of invitations: 'Come to him, the living stone, chosen and precious in God's sight."

Blessing:

"Grow in the grace and knowledge of our Lord and savior Jesus Christ. To Him be glory, both now and to the day of eternity. Amen."
(The blessing at the end of Peter's second letter.)

CHAPTER 12

Jesus All Along

I do not want you to be unaware, brothers
and sisters, that our ancestors were all under
a cloud, and all passed through the sea, and
all were baptized into Moses in the cloud
and in the sea, and all ate the same spiritual
food, and all drank the same spiritual drink.
For they drank from the spiritual rock that
followed them and the rock was Christ.
—1 Corinthians 10:1–4 NIV

It was a baptism that took forty years. When the children of Israel emerged from that long journey through the sea and the cloud of the presence of God, the old ones were dead. Those who had grown up in slavery were gone, and so was the sense of slavery and escape. Those who remained were children of the promise on their way home.

For forty years, they had lived on manna. They had drunk the water from the living rock. What happened to them physically was an illustration of a much greater reality. They were changed in the inner person—or at least they had the opportunity to be changed.

They all ate manna, the bread of the journey, fresh every morning and impossible to store. When there was no water to be found, they all (two million or more) drank water from the rock. By day, they traveled under the cloud of the presence of God; every night, the pillar of fire could be seen over the tent of meeting.

They knew they were in the presence of glory. They knew their God was God indeed, almighty and holy; Yahweh, El Shaddai. They knew he was one.

Now Paul says that rock, that presence in the wilderness was Christ. He was there all along.

(He was writing to a group of believers in Greece, and so he used the Greek word for Messiah, anointed one. He used "Christ.")

Is holiness a place you go, the destination of a life's journey? Lots of religions and lots of people think so, and so there are pilgrimages to Lourdes, to Benares, and to Mecca. There are standing stones and sacred groves all over the world.

But here, the idea is just the opposite—in the form of the cloud by day and the pillar of fire by night, the Shekhinah, the glory of God, followed them. Holiness followed them. Under the cloud and through the parting sea and through a wilderness where no water could be found, they had been fol-lowed and fed and cared for.

The experience in the wilderness was a spiritual journey even greater than the geographical one. The support was spiritual as well as physical.

"They drank from the rock that followed them," Paul wrote. "And that rock was Christ."

Here is the mystery revealed, the great secret disclosed.

Christ, the Savior of the world, was present in the wilderness.

The Persian diviner, Balaam, saw him from afar and said, "Their God is among them like a king."

He was there all along, the rock, the water, the Shekinah, the glory of God; it was Christ in action. But no one knew him, but not until he had a human face and not until Jesus could he begin to be known. The mountain where Moses went to meet God was so holy that if anyone touched it, they died. But now, the holiness that could not be touched is here among us as Balaam foresaw.

We've studied and thought about the picture of the rock in the lives of Jacob, Moses, Isaiah, and David and put them together with the conversation between Jesus and Peter:

"Who do you say that I am?"
"You are the Messiah, the Son of
the Living God!"

"I tell you, flesh and blood has not revealed this to you, but my Father, which is in heaven. And I tell you, you are, and on this rock I will build my church."

Still, we thought, maybe we're reaching. After all, a metaphor should be pushed only so far. Then we read from 1 Corinthians, and we felt as though we had hit the bull's-eye!

There are some mixed images here—the rock, the rock that followed, and the rock from which they drank. But remember, it's not a literary device that concerns us; it is a great truth, a truth outside human explanation but within human experience.

Task:

Watch for the places where Christ is blessing and following you. He was not a holy one in a holy place but a living presence in their midst—in our midst!

Blessing:

May the God of glory fill, protect, and amaze you right now and forever more. Amen.

CHAPTER 13

THE VOICE AT THE END OF THE WORLD

And the one seated on the throne said,
"See, I am making all things new."
Also he said, "Write this, for these
things are trustworthy and true."
Then he said to me,
"It is done!
I am Alpha and Omega,
the beginning and the end.
To the thirsty I will give water as a gift
from the spring of the water of life."
—Revelation 21:5–6 NIV

I am the Alpha and the Omega,
the first and the last,
the beginning and the end.

"It is I, Jesus, who sent my angel to you
with this testimony for the churches.
I am the root and the descendant of David,

the bright and morning star."
—Revelation 22:13, 16 NIV

This chapter contains no reference at all to a rock. So why is it included here? If you've followed the study so far, the answer is easy. The "rock" has never been about a rock; it has always been about a truth so large and wonderful that it couldn't be adequately communicated in ordinary ways. Now, this truth is clear, and it can be declared. It is Jesus, the beginning and the end, the origin and destination of humankind, and the reality underlying reality. Now, we know what the "rock" means.

The revelation to John is filled with complex and powerful symbols that talk about truths that are beyond the experience of the one who received them. For centuries, those who read this book have been intrigued and bewildered. But at the end of all this dazzling imagery, a picture comes into focus. We see Jesus, and his words ring out plain and clear. He uses the name he had on Earth, the name of the child he once became, and the name which he carries into eternity. He says:

> "It is I, Jesus. I am the root and offspring of David, the bright and morning star."

John, the beloved disciple, now grown to great old age, was in exile on an island in the Adriatic

Sea. It was a barren place, and he was standing on a rocky shore, alone and oblivious to the vast sea and the sky around him. His eyes were filled with a vision of the new heaven and the new earth—a reality yet to be. He saw the city of God, built on a vast foundation of precious stone, and he saw an angel, measuring the city with a measuring stick made of gold. He heard a voice ringing from the throne of heaven. It announces:

> "Look?! God's dwelling place is now among the people…" (Revelation 21:10 NIV)

It is a voice he recognizes. It goes on.

> "Look! I am coming soon! Blessed is the one who keeps the words of the prophecy written in this scroll." (Revelation 22:7 NIV)
> It is done!
> I am Alpha and Omega, the beginning and the end.
> To the thirsty, I will give water as a gift from the spring of the water of life.
> I will be their God and they will be my children."

The reality replaces the image. This is the real water from the rock, seen for what it represents; the life that flows from Messiah/Christ.

Think now of another old man, standing in a rocky place, four centuries before the time of Christ. His sandals are undone beside him because he stands in a holy place. Before him, a multitude waits restlessly. They are desperate, facing imminent death from dehydration.

The man speaks to the rock as he has been told to do. Then, because he is desperate too, he strikes it as well, with the staff that is the symbol of his authority. The dry rock splits, and water pours out. It gushes over the feet of the startled people. It soaks their clothing as they kneel to scoop it into their mouths. It floods the dusty ground and turns it into mud. By now, they are cheering, dizzy with the realization that they will live.

It is the same water and the same source of life from the one who underlies all creation—all thirst and all quenching of thirst, the origin and the destination of all things.

There was another witness important for us to hear. She was a woman, without name or reputation. She didn't even have a legitimate place in the Jewish world because she was a Samaritan. She was the woman at the well. She was an outcast in her own community, who came to draw water in the heat of the day when no one else was there.

Jesus spoke to her, as no decent Jewish man should have done, and he drew her into a conversation about water. He asked her for a drink. She, no longer the focus of men's casual interest but only of their unending needs, was wary.

"How is it that you, a Jew, would even ask me for a drink?" she asked.

There was no one else there, and Jesus spoke to her as if she were the most important person he could meet.

"If you knew the gift of God," he said, "and who it is who asked you for a drink, you would ask him, and he would have given you living water."

She, no pushover for a smooth talking stranger, challenged him right back.

"Then are you greater than our ancestor Jacob, who gave us this well?"

Jesus took the question seriously.

"Everyone who drinks this water will be thirsty again, but those who drink the water I give will never be thirsty again."

And there was more.

"The water I will give will become a spring of water gushing up to eternal life."

The woman must had paused then and given him a long look. But she took the cue and treated it as it served her needs.

"All right, sir, then give me this water that I may never be thirsty or have to keep coming here to draw water."

And here is a recorded conversation of such intimacy and self-disclosure that it startles us. Jesus, no doubt speaking quietly and leaning close to her ear because this was her personal shame, told her all she had done and done wrong in her life. And she, no longer hiding in cynical repartee, realized that she was speaking to a prophet. She put to him a genuine question, the critical question that divides Samaritan from Jew. "Is holiness a place? Do we worship on this mountain or in Jerusalem as the Jews insist?"

The woman at the well, not a man and not a full Jew, would normally not have had any conversation at all with Jesus. But she became one of the first theologians of the New Testament, discussing with Jesus the nature of worshipping God. Jesus was making the shift from holy place and rule keeping to living worship in spirit and in truth.

"Woman," he said, "the time is coming when you will worship the Father, neither on this mountain nor in Jerusalem. God is Spirit and those who worship must worship in spirit and in truth."

Was there a hush as she took this in? She understood enough to venture.

"I know Messiah is coming, and when he comes, he will proclaim all things to us."

And Jesus answered the unspoken question, "I am he, the one who is speaking to you"

And the Lord of all creation, the one for whom all metaphor and all description fail, sat with one sad woman and made her glad.

The underlying reality—the Shekinah and the glory of God—is no longer coded as the rock but is now seen as who he is—the man who is God and the God who became man—Jesus Christ.

Task:

Watch for the outsider, the one who has ruined their life. Watch for the focus of God's love on that person. Jesus, "God-made man, the wish that worked," came for that one.

Blessing:

"Look, I am coming soon! Blessed is the one who keeps the words of the prophecy written in this scroll" (Revelation 22:7 NIV).

ABOUT THE AUTHOR

Merle Cooper pastored Methodist churches in New York, New Jersey, and California. He is a retired Air Force chaplain who has served in New York, California, Germany, Thailand, and the Azores, Portugal. He holds degrees from Penn State, New York Theological Seminary, and San Francisco Theological Seminary.

Charlotte Cooper graduated from UCLA and California State University, Sacramento. She is an encaustic painter. Before she became a working artist, she partnered with her husband in ministry and also taught special education.